LIMITED DUTY OFFICER (LDO)

The Motivation, the Process, the End-State
Goal in Becoming a Mustang

Lieutenant Roel "Ro" Rosalez, MJA

abbott press

Abbott Press books may be ordered through booksellers or by contacting:

Abbott Press
1663 Liberty Drive
Bloomington, IN 47403
www.abbottpress.com
Phone: 1 (866) 697-5310

ISBN: 978-1-4582-2150-6 (sc)
ISBN: 978-1-4582-2149-0 (e)

Library of Congress Control Number: 2017917368

Print information available on the last page.

Abbott Press rev. date: 11/14/2017

Contents

Foreword

I want to thank and give all the glory to my God, the father of my Savior, the Lord Jesus Christ for getting me to this point and never failing me with mercy and grace, even when I don't deserve all these blessings. Second, to my wife and two boys. You have put up with so much from this career and it is still not over with. Over 12 PCS moves and 14 schools, there are several others who are going to mirror your lives, although I am glad you were given this strength to continue this path with me. Let's dolphin dive into this book! I love you all! To all the Shipmates, Marines and Civilians who encouraged, assisted, and guided to me up to this point, thank you! You know who you are! To those of you who said I would never get here, questioned me, and stated I was too young, apparently, the board and most importantly the Lord thought differently.

Mustang / Limited Duty Officer

W hy are Limited Duty Officers (LDOs) called "Mustangs"? It is known that Mustangs are wild horses who are hard to tame, but after several tries, the Mustang is broken and it is ridden like a normal bred horse. Although, with Mustangs you must be very careful, because at any moment they can revert to their old wild ways. This is the same of LDOs, they are from the enlisted ranks and have crossed over to the commissioned ranks, which requires them to adapt to the lifestyle of an Officer and perform accordingly both personally and professionally. However, like wild Mustangs, they can revert to their old wild ways.

The LDOs are Subject Matter Experts in their Naval occupational field. Currently, there are ever changing numbers of designators, which are filled with Sailors just like you, who came from the enlisted ranks and had that same aspiration you currently have. So what do they do? As someone once told me, "LDOs don't complain, they just plug holes". Sure enough, that is the best analogy I can explain what an LDO does. In Navy terms, they are subject matter experts in their fields of occupation.

Sailors either love LDOs or hate LDOs, but LDOs

should never bring the persona of being feared as that is not what we should be instilling into juniors, superiors or peers. LDOs should be the leaders everyone looks for to help solve a problem, someone easily relied upon when a challenge arises, one who speaks and the Triad listens because they know and value their reliability and wisdom. Although not the most scholarly of the Commissioned Officers, we are the ones who are able to tame a situation as needed and at the appropriate level. An LDO has no intention but the best for the command, the Navy, and the country. As in any profession there are a few under performers and LDOs are no exception, but the vast majority of LDOs are at the ready to ably assist the command, the mission, and their shipmates. At times, they may come on strong when they are trying to get their point across, and certain personnel may not agree with LDOs responses, but they tend to do what is right rather than what is popular because they want to do what is best for the mission.

Why am I writing this book?

Now that I have gone over the reasoning of why they call LDOs "Mustangs", let's get right to the point. If you bought this book, it's because you are currently in the enlisted ranks and want to become a Limited Duty Officer (LDO) or someone sparked the idea at you, maybe one of your family members is a LDO. Although, this book cannot promise you selection on the new accession board, this book will give you different pointers on what can make your record more appealing to the board. There have been many from the enlisted ranks who became LDOs in the U.S. Navy, although there have been more personnel who have applied and were not selected. Many personnel who always wanted to be an LDO, but never wanted to apply. Either because they didn't know if they were good enough, or maybe they did not want to face rejection. Bottom line, they will never know!

Not everyone is meant to be an LDO, but several of you are meant to be a Mustang! Some of you may try once and get selected, some of you may try several times and never get selected, but at least you tried and the Lord has a purpose for you somewhere in the Navy, maybe as the next MCPON, CMDCM, Chief or LPO, but he has a purpose. Some will never try, and come to realize this was one of your biggest regrets, once the opportunity is past. I will never forget what I said on my personal statement section of my application of why I wanted to be an LDO. "I wanted to give the same aspirations, goals and dreams I currently have to other Sailors in the future." Well, this is part of wanting to give back to future generations, and throughout the chapters, you will read about other portions of my application. People gave me pointers since I was an E-1 and some people didn't even realize what they were doing, others just threw gasoline on this fire inside of me, which I call the fire of motivation.

A little background on myself to let you know where I stand and where I started. Three juvenile felonies, one Driving While Intoxicated arrest, hearing waiver, marijuana use waiver, cocaine use waiver and a subpar ASVAB score for a 19-year-old kid from South Texas with a child on the way that I didn't even know about. If the odds were against someone it was me and I was happy to just join the Navy. All these items are brought up for the reason to give you some motivation in why you even bought this book. Your odds might be as bad, maybe even worse, or maybe you are clean as a whistle but determination is the most important part of the process, the only person that can stop you from accomplishing this goal, is yourself. Look at yourself in the mirror, that's right, take pause and look at yourself in the mirror. What do you really want? Picture yourself in the rank you hope to achieve. My goal in boot camp was to one day retire as a First Class Petty Officer, which is an honorable rank and many of my best friends have retired at that rank. Over the years, my life took a different direction, family responsibilities, different job assignments, financial requirements, different leaders, changes in policies, ideas which could contribute to my profession. These different items shaped my new goal of becoming a commissioned officer. Do you want that same goal? Do you want to put in some extra effort and sacrifice some time and relaxation to join the Commissioned officer ranks as a Mustang? Maybe you wonder how this person you call a DIVO or Department Head can even be your boss? You know you could do a better job if only you were in that position but lack of rank is holding you back. You can be that DIVO and you can be that Department Head. It starts now, working toward that goal, it doesn't matter if you have one year in service or if this is your last year of eligibility. You will have to sacrifice and you will have to receive support from superiors, peers, and family. This book is written from the perspective of a married with children type of Mustang who needed no extra motivation to conquer this goal. That's right no extra motivation was needed, when you are an E-3 in the early 2000s, have a family of three, paying child support on another and have everything to lose with my family. If you are in this predicament, or maybe in a different one, which only you can understand, but you still have the dream of becoming a commissioned Naval Officer; guess what, it is not too late!

In the long run, you have to decide what you want: an enlistment of four years and an honorable discharge and go on to the U.S. Navy Reserves and become an LDO, or decide to stay in and progress to the top of the enlisted ranks as a Master Chief make that decision and convert to that subject matter expert in your field, becoming a Limited Duty Officer, a Mustang, an LDO. Imagine... Ensign _____(your first and last name), that's exactly how I was thinking, but the road looked cloudy and it seemed like the sunrays never shined on me, but I was never going to give up on that dream until the U.S. Navy advised me to give up. Fortunately, I only submitted once and the Navy said my dream of becoming a Mustang was now a reality. In this book, I will guide you and answer many of the questions I had and I was too scared to ask or did not have someone that was personally close enough to ask.

How bad do you want it?

You must reach deep down inside of yourself and figure out how much you want to be an LDO. If you want something bad enough, work toward that goal, everything is obtainable. Don't get me wrong, for some this will be an easy task and they will obtain commission on the first try, others will be trying for three, four years, maybe even longer, but this is where you start deciding how many sacrifices you are willing to accept to become an LDO. This is not only a choice for yourself, but a choice for your whole family. The support must come from them if you want to succeed. Yes, that is correct, your spouse and your children will need to come forward and understand what you are about to get everyone involved in. Yes, the commission brings more money to the family, a sense of accomplishment and much more responsibility. With all of this comes more sacrifices, hard work, expectations from superiors, hard decisions for your subordinates, and even envy, jealously from people you never expected. You are correct, just because you obtain that commission, the hard work does not stop and if anything, it means you will be working harder than ever before and you are going to have to face challenges and responsibilities which you never expected. For some these challenges may provide leverage to bolster their career, for others its constructive criticism from Commanding Officers or Flag Officers. I mention these issues, because if you are running into issues like these at work, you will not be able to take on these challenges without the support from your family.

Don't get me wrong, there will be plenty who become LDOs and will never have support from their family, who will be good officers, but will have a tough time at work and will not be able to fully commit themselves to God, country and service. Which means, they fall short of what they promised to do when they accepted their commission. After saying all of this, how bad do you want it? Remember, this not just about yourself, not just about your family, but the men and women you will lead, make decisions for, some right, some wrong, and some you will always second guess yourself on. This will not happen overnight, and it will not happen without any extra work from you and the request of blessings from above. As I mention to Sailors all the time, if all you did during the first few years of your career was to conduct business at the bare minimum or as we know it being a 3.0 Sailor, then what makes you think the selection board will select you over the next Sailor. How much did you commit, which will reflect on your evaluations? Again, I say, this will not be an overnight decision and you cannot expect for it to be an overnight selection. You start working for this goal as a young Petty Officer Second Class and as of lately, I have seen some Sailors holding the rank of Petty Officer Third Class attending LDO power point presentations at roadshows. In other words, you are never too young to start working toward this goal. Along the same route, do I believe you might be too late in your career when applying for this program? No, just as there are Sailors who apply and are selected for the LDO program in their first year of eligibility, you too can apply for the first time and be selected on your last year of eligibility. Again, what have you done over the years to accomplish this goal? Remember, if you have good work ethics, you are not going to change those work ethics overnight. I have seen Mustangs who are burned out and that fire that was once burning inside of them, just ran out of fuel and they are waiting for that twilight tour and the next few years to pass by. For some Sailors, the fire never goes out, some Sailors not only want to be commissioned but want the Eagle too. That's right, the rank of Captain, but we will talk about that in the next few chapters. Getting back to the subject, you must be ready with sustained superior performance reflecting your evaluations, qualifications, volunteer hours, special skills, awards, and a generally well-rounded Sailor, as well as being an ambassador to the community on behalf of the U.S. Navy. All of these values are examples of your application but you should also present yourself, in a manner that exhibits your application on this new and difficult challenge of becoming an LDO. In the next couple of sections, I will explain why the application is so important, the understanding of how you have to present yourself and knowing the inside and out of the OPNAVINST 1420 series.

How long have you been thinking about this?

I have been commissioned for a little over eight years, and over the years, I have met with plenty of Sailors who mention in passing that they think about applying for LDO. I can honestly say I have talked to over 100 Sailors stating they want to be an LDO. Unfortunately, only 13 of them have followed through and submitted an officer package. All 13 were selected! I bring this up for the reason to remind you that many Sailors want to achieve those goals, except many of those same Sailors do not want to put in the effort to meet those goals. If the case was that easy, everyone would be an LDO.

So how long have you been thinking about this goal? Some of you have been thinking about this goal since boot camp, some of you may have started considering this program since you were an E-5, some of you just started when you picked up this book. Does it matter? I believe it does, for two simple reasons, the longer the timeframe, the more homework you have done on this program and the better prepared you will be. Second, the more iterations or drafts of the application you have completed, the more errors you will catch and the better finished product you will have.

I have seen some Sailors submit their applications within a three-month timeframe of working on the application and they are selected, but if you are like me, you have to work on your application for years. Sounds crazy huh! The reason I worked on it for so long was that I did not want to give the board an excuse to tell me "NO"! As a matter of fact, I wanted to make sure all my ducks were in a row and that there was no doubt I was selected the first year I applied. I felt so confident, I had purchased my butter bars the day I submitted my application. I knew the program in and out, received very little guidance until weeks before I submitted the application, and no matter what was against me, I knew the Lord was with me so who could possibly defeat me. I will be honest with you and the day I became serious in wanting to be an officer was the day I selected for Petty Officer Second Class. When my peers called me and asked me to go out with them to some local bars and celebrate the advancement results, my answer was simply telling them I was going to start working on my LDO package. They thought of me as this looney tune Sailor who was letting this advancement get to my head. I was just thinking of all these famous athletes as that was the best analogy I could come up with. Did Michael Jordan, Joe Montana, Nolan Ryan all become overnight sensations. No, they worked over time to become the athletes they were destined to be. I was simply looking at it in these terms as well. When someone is passionate about a certain topic, occupation, a sport, or even a hobby, they are going to excel because they are passionate about that specific item; and if you happen to fail at what you are passionate about, you will get back up and make sure you succeed. What happens when you are not truly passionate about said topic? It's a 50/50 situation and if you fail, you just put that behind you and continue onto the next topic or item you wish to achieve, hopefully becoming an LDO is a topic you are deeply passionate about.

Toilet

Toilet? What the heck is he talking about? Well, what is the place you know you will be visiting every day of your life. That's right the toilet! So, what does that have to do with you becoming an LDO? This is just a pointer or advice based from my experience, what I used to do, and that was to keep my most recent rough draft of my application and a copy of the most recent chapter of the LDO instruction on the back of the toilet. Yes, so much so, my wife would give me grief for having these documents there. I would comb the instruction and the draft application daily, again, to make sure it was ready for board viewing. Remember what I mentioned when I started working this application, the night I was selected to Second Class Petty Officer, which was June of 2003 and I submitted the application around August of 2007. So, for four years my wife had to put up with this and I know for a fact she has no complaints on this matter at this moment. Please advise your spouses, this process does not stop the minute you are selected, as you will be applying for other programs later in your career and don't forget that SWO pin or warfare device.

If you have some other location where you have private

or quiet time make sure a copy of each of these forms are there. Along with having a copy where ever you go and even in your work space. I learned this from a movie and a shipmate from many years ago. The movie was about a teacher who was trying to teach underprivileged teenagers Algebra and to make sure they did not fail, he gave three textbooks to one student. One for home, one for class, and one for the locker, just in case he forgot the one textbook for class. He wanted to make sure the student had no excuses for failing. The same lesson I learned from an MA2, who would not stop walking around with a Master-At-Arms distance learning textbook when he was going up for MA1. He had taken the exam and failed the in-rate portion miserably, but had done great with the overall Navy portion. He made up his mind that this would never happen again was going to ensure he would take every opportunity to study for the next six months. He scored 97 percentile above his peers and made MA1 the following cycle. This is where I discovered that this studying of a specific subject can never fail, so I ensured I always studied the instruction, the previous boards characteristics, my application and now you have the thought process in this book as well. Let's move on to the application process.

Application process

Okay, you are ready, or are you? In the following pages, I will be discussing different parts of the application process. Getting to this point in your career is a big step in what you really want out of your career. To some applicants, this may seem like the most difficult obstacle you will be encountering, while others the application process will seem rather easy. None the less, it will be a lengthy process that may take 16 months or like me it took 26 months from start to finish. That's right, I took the Chief's exam for LDO purposes in January 2007, submitted my application in October 2007, notified in February 2008 that I was selected and was finally commissioned in February 2009. That's a long time, but if you stay consistent and persistent with the application, you will be wearing those butter bars soon enough. To get this through your heads, some of you will talk about applying for a long portion of your career but will never finish the process. I have met plenty of Sailors in this situation and one of the reasons I wrote this book is to prevent from this happening as much as possible and to motivate you to submit the application. Don't be one of those Sailors who never applies but just talks about it. If you are falling into this category and your timeframe to submit an application is starting to decrease, read the rest of this book which will help motivate you and provide you tips to ease the application process.

Don't get confused on when you can apply

⟋⟍

Short and sweet, know the instructions (OPNAV 1420.1(series)) inside and out, if you are ready to lead Sailors because you feel this is one of your positive traits you will be bringing to the Wardroom, then you must know programs. Both inside and outside the Navy, some programs might be around only for a few years and some programs will be around for decades. If you are going to try to lead Sailors, you will be required to be squared away with your own wants and needs. In other words, if you don't know the officer application requirements yourself, how are you going to lead other people with similar goals and aspirations. You do not have to be an expert at every topic but you will be required to know where to get the information for Sailors. Throughout this book, I relate stories of challenges, situations or problems rounding up at the end how they relate to the LDO program. So, on this topic, knowing when you can apply is the first order of business. Understand the one year in rate requirement as a First-Class Petty Officer (FCPO) and know the years of service regardless of rank for either the LDO or the CWO program. I have encountered peers, as a FCPO, where the said peer was the Command Career Counselor (CCC) for the installation and they are advising me I could not take the Chief Petty Officer Exam for LDO purposes because I am required to have one year time in rate. Little did he know, the one-year time in rate is when the application is due, which is usually October 1st of every year. I had to sit down with him and show him in the instructions where I was authorized. I end up finding out, that this CCC had turned three people away the previous year including himself. Because I have been confrontational most of my life, I choose not to be anymore, but when you know you are right and an argument commences, it is better to show instructions, procedures, or guidance than to be going back and forth with a wall, especially when this decision makes an impact on your career.

Do your homework, don't listen to other people

What exactly does the title of this section mean? Well, it goes hand-in-hand with the previous section, know what the board will be impressed with in order to select you and only rely on your mentors and those who have been there before you. It is amazing, when people are teenagers, they tend to believe that their parents don't know any better, they are too old to understand and obviously the parents cannot understand what they are going through in these teenage years due to the parents showing them no proof of facts. Yet, the parents are usually their best bet as to who these teenagers should be listening too. At the same time, if you have been in the Navy long enough, you notice how some Sailors tend to listen to their peers, or superiors without ever referencing an instruction, lessons learned, standard operating procedures, etc. No proof is ever shown and the Sailors just tend to go with this hearsay information, which is totally the opposite of what they were saying or arguing about during their teenage years, almost hypocrisy! Why do I bring this up? The officer application instruction is great to know as I mentioned before, and this book you are reading is another great reference to understand from a LDOs perspective, but what else can help you? Look at previous years LDO administrative boards and see what type of people the board has been selecting. Talk to different LDOs throughout the year, don't wait until June of the year you are applying to start talking to local Mustangs. It doesn't always have to be a mentor with in your rate, you might find a mentor from another rate. Do that homework! But more than likely you always find the same questions being asked involving the programs. You see, I love to sit down with LDO applicants because no one ever sat down with me until I started applying. At that moment, they just advised me to change a few items on my application and they knew I was a shoe in for selection. Why? Because I had done my homework on the application? They didn't have to be bothered much and all of them gave me the sit-down interview saying you will be selected, so start thinking now how you are going to lead departments, work with senior enlisted personnel (crusty old Master Chiefs), touch up on programs which will help out your junior personnel and be ready to have a scholarly conversation as a Department Head (none the less as a LTJG) on a Nuclear Aircraft Carrier with post-command Captains and Commanders.

Is this what you really want? You will have to be sleeping, eating and working the LDO application during your time off. As mentioned before, there are some LDOs who are just gifted and can get the application together in a couple of weeks, but I wanted to make sure I was not turned away on try number one. So, I did my homework on FY-07, FY-08 selectees and applicants who were not selected and the first time was a charm for me in FY-09. All this extra work was worth it, as I reflect back a little over ten years ago when I was taking the CPO exam for LDO purposes.

Get a mentor

It doesn't matter how many years you have in, it is always good to bounce ideas off someone. Someone you can trust, someone you know will not laugh at your ideas and even have similar goal oriented work ethics you have. Someone who can be honest with you and not lie to you about the process. There is not much needed to put two and two together on this topic. All LDOs say the exact same thing in their application process, you are probably putting the same wording in your application that I am about to mention involving leadership. I have read plenty of packages stating about wanting to give Sailors the leadership guidance, mentorship, helping them out with their goals of becoming leaders in the U.S. Navy. Some might have used the wording from previous LDO packages which were submitted and others come out with their own unique words. None the less, each package talks about leadership in their application and what they are bringing into the Wardroom, as if leadership is a new trait being introduced to the Wardroom and there aren't enough leaders. I mention this not to mock the leadership mentality, but to remind you as a soon to be Mustang, and even for you old Mustangs who are reading this book that part of that leadership requires to look over future LDO packages. I mention this due to having an open-door policy, plenty of newly inspired Sailors come to me asking questions about the program, which reminds me of my years of aspiring to be an LDO, which is also part of the reason I am writing this book. The issue I have is when I ask them if their LDO Department Head is aware of their goal to be an LDO and the answer is no. Don't get me wrong, it is up to the Sailor to notify his/her chain of command, but Mustangs need to advertise this program to the fullest.

When obtaining a mentor, you need to be aware of what you need from them, be ready with questions about the program, career, personal and I have even had people want to talk spiritually. This mentor is not a person, you only want to vent to about your day at work, or brag about your accomplishments, this is a leader who you aspire to be like and you will soon be walking in their footsteps. At the same time be mindful, because there are still plenty of Mustangs that will take two to three hours of their day to talk about the program they realize has helped them out in their career, yet will stay after work to make up those two to three hours' worth of work as if the Navy pays overtime. Who or what people miss out on those two to three hours with that LDO while you go home and spend time on your application? The Mustang's family! What I am trying to explain is that, it is an ever-evolving cycle which passes through Navy generations as you will be expected to help junior Sailors out as well. You see this journey that you love so much, starts when you apply and it only goes up in speed when you get selected and each rank after that. The problem is we don't know how much gas we have in the tank and how far we are going to be able to go in this career.

Don't wait until the last minute

W hat do I mean by waiting until the last minute, well in this program there are several different places where you can wait until the last minute. The first process in where you can wait until the last minute with the LDO program involves the time in service requirement, which as of 2017, the program limitation is eight to 14 years. What I am trying to explain is if you know you are LDO material and this has been an end state goal for you, don't wait until the last one or two years to apply if you are eligible at the eight year mark. This goes back to how you can procrastinate on a goal that you want. Remember, there is always someone hungrier than you are or someone who wants the same goal as you do and they are willing to put in the extra hours of work or sacrifice a couple of hours of sleep to accomplish this goal. So why wait until year 13 or 14, or even year 12? Here is the best sound advice I can give you, get the application completed as soon as possible and if you must wait another year to be eligible then update the application the following year, but don't wait around for the whole application to be submitted a couple of months prior to the yearly deadline of October 1st. As mentioned with my history of when

I started working on my application. It was the day I was notified of my promotion to Master-At-Arms Second Class Petty Officer, I was invited to go celebrate at the local bars. Instead, I advised my shipmates, I had bought a six pack of beer and that I was going to start working on my LDO application/package and they said I was crazy. I guess I am not that crazy now, huh? That is the example of sacrificing one night with friends to start on the end state goal of becoming an LDO. After several drafts, three different commands, I was finally eligible to apply and I was not running around like a mad man trying to get the application together on the last minute. As I let everyone know who I mentor, this package was not a package to determine if it was good enough, but after years of building up my resume as a Military Police Officer, this package was to let the selection board know that I was ready. It was not a package to see if the board was going to determine if I was LDO ready, but their chance to finally tell me yes. You see, I was not a sitting duck during the first eight years of my career and I continue to not be one, I am always looking at how or what I need to do to succeed. By waiting around for the next day, the next week or even the next year to submit the LDO application is not one of the mindsets that will get you selected. Don't wait for the last minute to apply!

The second criteria I am talking about is waiting until the last minute was briefly mentioned in the previous paragraph. Don't wait until the last minute to decide that you want to apply, look for a mentor, put the application together, and look for board members. As I also mentioned in the previous paragraph, this type of procrastination will not get you selected. So, when is it too late to decide, never, it is never too late to apply nor is it too late to decide that you want to be an LDO. But I will say, if you know that this is what you want, then get it done early, don't procrastinate on the application, Sailors, and people in general, tend to procrastinate and say they will complete something later. I say this out of experience, this book is a perfect example as I thought about this approximately eight years ago, but I procrastinated for this long. That is approximately half of my career where I could have written this book, projected this motivation, helped other Sailors get selected and provided information for LDO selectees. We as professionals who are comfortable tend to procrastinate; don't be in that comfort zone, where you are satisfied with where you are. The Lord did not give you talent, to wait, you can be doing a lot of great things on this earth, for this country, for the Navy. Every year, besides completing the application, you should be improving your resume, your mind, your contribution to the Navy. I am not talking about volunteering for 20 collateral duties that you never touch, except to make your evaluations look better. I am talking about real contributions and this includes being well-rounded which will show on the application. You need to properly advertise yourself on the application to the board and to do this, you need to give yourself time to complete the application. There is a baseline floating around in emails to ensure you get the application done correctly. Here is an example of when you need to get the process complete. Again, this is a suggestion.

FY message is released ---- March
Application completed ------May
Board interviews conducted-------July
Commanding Officer process-----August
Confirmation of submission in Millington, TN-----September

You can adjust the above timeline as needed or as your command requires you to, but if you have your application ready, the timeline will not affect you. Bottom line --don't wait, always be ready!

The interview process

When it comes to the interview process, the best advice I can give you is to bring your "A" game. You see, I have been giving this advice for about a decade and only few listen, those few who did listen, just happened to be selected. When you go up for an interview, you never know what you are going to be asked, this is the only unknown in the whole process. You just never know, what an old crusty LDO on the other side of the table will ask, but the one truth that will come out of the board will let you know if you are ready. Think about this, on the other side of the table you will have three to four LDOs who will have 10 to 37 years of experience each, that's right, you can be looking at a combined 148 years of Naval experience. Are you ready to face that? How will you really know what they are going to ask--you won't. What you can do for the interview is: tell the truth, think about your answer before you speak, and walk into the interview room with a squared away uniform and ready to answer any question with confidence. Just don't go in to the board expecting to blow smoke at the LDO's and think you are going to get away with it. The rest you leave up to the Lord to handle. What I am getting at, is there is no one way that you will be able to handle the interview, very similar to the understanding that there will not be only one way that you will be able to handle an issue, a challenge, or a problem when you become an LDO. You simply must be prepared as best as possible, explain your answers from the experiences you have learned along the way and remember to think about your answers before you blurt them out. The majority of the questions which are asked during the local boards are never a right or wrong, yes or no answers, they are wanting to see how you answer the questions while holding onto your composure. This is the same mindset you will need, when you are being asked questions by your Commanding Officer or a Flag Officer and you need to answer without blurting the first thing that comes to mind, along with keeping your composure. You don't want to embarrass yourself, at the same time, know that no single local board or interview process is perfect. The only thing you can do is try your hardest, just like you do at your job. This is just a similar situation in what you will be facing in the fleet, or at your command once you become a commissioned officer; you will not be a perfect LDO, but you will try your hardest to do so in everything you do.

What will help me?

―――――〰――――――

There are several items which can assist and prepare you to become selected for the LDO designator you are applying for. I will go over a few key items, which can assist you in being selected, although these are not all the factors, these are what the board will be looking at in selecting the best of the best. It might seem impossible to receive the maximum amount of points at the board on each of these topics, although you can be well-rounded. What do I mean by being well-rounded? The issues the local boards or even the selection board do not want to see is someone who has 20 collateral duties and promotable evaluations, nor someone who has over 1000 community service hours in two years, yet does not have a warfare qualification. Now let's get into these topics and see what you are exceling in and where you are lacking, none-the-less, remember who the person is who can stop you from being selected. Only yourself!

Sustained superior performance

There is nothing better to have on your record before a selection board than sustained superior performance.

This can only be confirmed through your evaluations with those early promotes denoted on those evaluations. There are several types of Sailors in the Navy, those that have always worked hard since day one and those that realize the Navy is not a bad gig and decide to change their ways and work hard once they are given responsibility. Remember, that the board can go back to your E-5 evaluations, so for those of you who are reading this and are below this rank does not mean that you don't have to worry about your evaluations. Instead start setting yourself up for success by having a good work ethic and working hard at every task that you are given. This way you don't have to start learning how to work hard at a later time in your career. You see, once you discover a certain trait such as a good work ethic, it is pretty much impossible to place it in your mind that you will, from one day to the next, turn into a dirt bag. If anything, that is the biggest issue with LDOs, they have this little spot inside of them that will never let them think, say or do, the words "I don't care". Once that happens, I would say it is time for them to retire. Chances are, true LDOs will never really want to retire, they more than likely, were twice a failure of selection and forced to retire. Your evaluations need to be ready to be presented to the board and just like all the other topics I will be mentioning in this section, this one is the one that needs to be above par. The more competitive you are with your evaluations, the better; especially if you are receiving those early promotions, but don't feel bad if they are not all early promotions. To relieve your concerns about that one evaluation you might be worried about, I, myself, had a frocked E-6 transfer "Must Promote" evaluation and one regular E-6 "Must Promote" evaluation, all my remaining evaluations that went before the board were from when I was an E-5. That's right you are probably thinking, how did he get selected with two MP evaluations and don't forget that when I went up for LDO, the time in service requirements were from eight to 16 years for eligibility, which meant I was competing again Senior Chief Petty Officers. I will say this, the board can read through the garbage politics I had to go through. The board actually read my evaluation narratives where they noticed as an E-5, I had lead over 160 personnel at one time, maintained a budget worth over $350K, and noticed my main job titles were different for almost every assignment. Not every Sailor's career is perfect, but the board has been around for a long time and they know that at times politics comes into play and as LDOs, we overcome these politics even before we wear the title. I will finish this section with this, if you are working hard all your career and really doing what is best for the Navy, you are already acting like an LDO. Once they select you to be an LDO, that is just icing on the cake! The rest of these topics are not this complicated, some you must have, others are not required, but highly recommended.

PQS.

To best explain this section, get as many qualifications as you can for the betterment of the Navy and the mission. The majority of these will be qualifications within your rate, although at times, the command, the ship, the squadron or whatever unit you are attached to will need someone to step out of their rate and into an uncomfortable job. This situation I am explaining does not always happen, but if the opportunity presents itself, take it and run with it. Because if you don't take it, someone else will. You know what each of your rates entail and what qualifications make you competitive in your rate. But let me throw out a couple of other possibilities which you can take advantage of ……. master helmsman, officer of the deck underway, conning officer during replenishment for ships……maybe in an expeditionary unit you can cover boat officer, coxswain, gunner, mission commander, etc.; you get the idea. Get the qualifications, not only for your professional growth, but to favorably enhance the mission.

Warfare qualifications

The more the merrier, but it does not mean that five warfare qualifications will automatically get you selected. Don't get me wrong, they cannot hurt and just like qualifications in the previous section, if the opportunity arises seize it! But there is way more to being selected than warfare qualifications. To balance this out, if your record shows up at the board with no warfare qualification and you had the opportunity, but failed to qualify, then that will look bad. For example, if you have been on three ships, but have never received at least one warfare qualification if not two depending on your rate and the type of ship, then you might be lacking. If you have more qualifications, it can never hurt you, but I have seen one Sailor who had five warfare qualification and was never selected for LDO and Chief Petty Officer. If you have never had the opportunity at a command to obtain a warfare qualification, then the board might understand, although, think about it from the board's perspective. What Sailor has served for eight to 14 years in the Navy and never been at a command that has a warfare qualification program? Almost every command has a warfare qualification program except

Naval Installations Command, which is also known as shore duty and everyone deserves shore duty, but for 14 straight years, is a bit too much.

Community Service

This is not the more the merrier, but a balance you must understand and not cross the line where you are thinking that 1,000 hours of community service or volunteer hours in one or two years will help you get selected. Community service is a great opportunity to help the community where you live or work, but the Navy has progressed this great service into a monster. You must realize that community service helps an applicant when he can be a well-rounded Sailor that handles all aspects of his job with sustained superior performance, community service, some college, some collateral duties, but a balance, not a spear in just one direction. Striving for a Military Outstanding Volunteer Service Medal (MOVSM) is a good goal to strive for, but again, not an absolute requirement to be selected for LDO. My best advice: don't overdo it with volunteer service hours.

Awards

Some commands and rates give out chest candy in abundance, while others hold back on awards. Why? I don't know, it happens to be the situation, but again, awards will not be the end all be all. I went into the selection board with three Navy/Marine Corps (N/MC) Achievement Medals and one N/MC Commendation Medal, which I thought was pretty good for eight and a half years in the Navy. But once I went through Mustang University in

Newport, RI with my awards, I noticed LDOs with four N/MC Commendation Medals, four N/MC Achievement Medals or LDOs with Meritorious Service Medals or Joint Meritorious Service Medals, which set me off my tracks. This is who I was competing against at one point! Do awards help? Yes, but if you have three medals for valid tours or achievements that were earned, that is a lot better than having six medals for citations that the board can see right through and say "next".

Education

This is a topic which I hold dear to my heart, because of the education I went to the board with. Degrees are not required for LDOs, but they are recommended, so remember this for those of you who still have years before they apply. If you are missing a few classes for an associate or bachelor degree, then get those classes done. That sheepskin on the wall does wonders, even for LDOs, so strive for that degree. If you don't have a degree, it is not the end of the world and you can make up for it in other sections of the application as I mentioned before, it is not a requirement, but a recommendation. I went into the selection board with my application stating my Master Degree was completed and I was taking courses for my PhD. Remember, someone is always hungrier than you are! What will you present to the board?

Navy Enlisted Classification (NECs) Codes

This topic is very much like the PQS topic and the qualifications which influence your rate. New NECs are being implemented every year and majority of them stick around your career once you receive them. Some personnel like to receive several NECs, which is never a bad situation, especially if you are planning to become an LDO, which will only make you a well-rounded LDO. Other Sailors, have received an NEC and stayed in the same job for the next 10 years, which will eventually keep you bottled up in one specific area of your rate. Bottom line is, I have seen Sailors get selected for LDO with one, two, three, six NECs and I have also seen Sailors get selected with zero, so there is no right or wrong number of NECs to have on your record. As always, if the opportunity arises to obtain an NEC, take it, run with it, and show that you will work as hard as possible while working with that NEC. Then you can say "next please"!

Collateral duties

This topic is similar to the volunteer/community hours topic, which I previously mentioned. Don't go out there and take 20 collateral duties, which you don't touch all year, with the expectation of placing them on your evaluation. I have seen this too often over my career and collateral duties have been overlooked as one of the most important criteria of a Sailor's evaluation. I am not saying this is of little importance, I am just saying that I personally know if one person who has 10 collateral duties on his evaluation, the chances of him/her taking care of all those collateral duties are slim. So please do not believe you can fake your evaluations and make the selection board believe you are taking care of "X" number collateral duties. That would only mean you don't have a job and are a collateral duty guru. However, do not ignore collateral duties, they are beneficial in helping a

Sailor grow in organizational leadership, maturing the Sailor in certain Navy programs, and assisting the Sailor in leading other Sailors, which he/she might not get from their normal jobs. There just must be a balance.

Hard Duty

Quick and easy, don't go shore to shore to shore duty and think you will get promoted to Captain. Take the hard duties and guess what, some of those duties might end up being shore duty. Some of these shore duties will be recruiter, RDC, and instructor duty, but there are also plenty of sea duties in almost every rate. It may not be what you want, but you need to understand, if you want to become an LDO, you should take the hard duties that no one else wants to take. You see, the board can determine the chances of a person changing their work ethics, their priority of taking on the hardest duty once they are selected to become an Ensign are slim. The real chance is that this person who is selected to become an LDO will probably continue with the same type of hard working mindset. So, take on those hard duties and excel at every job!

Should I apply or not and Why?

If you bought this book, this should not even be a question? Unfortunately, some people are trying to determine whether to "cross over to the dark side" or not. What is this "dark side" the majority of your leadership or peers are talking about? That's right! Most of the people who say this are intentionally or unintentionally trying to put some fear into you. If you think about it, what is the "dark side"; it is an analogy of the dark side from the Star Wars movie franchise. The scary side, the mean side, the side you want to lose in that battle at the end of the movie. If you really think about it, you also bought this book to determine when to apply for the program. This is not an easy process, but you should know what you want especially if you are leading Sailors. Being in the Wardroom is not for everyone, although you should think if this is really going to be for you. Why is it that you have applied in the past, did the reasoning change? Whatever the reason is that you are applying should be coming from you, not from anyone else. Additionally, whatever you are thinking about why you are applying should go into your personal statement section of the application. As an old shipmate once stated to me, we all joined the Navy for different reasons, some because they had no guidance, no directions, no parents, not enough money to go to college, you were trying to start a new direction in life, people were financially dependent on you, a chance to travel the world and the list goes on and on. The same goes for applying for LDO, there are many reasons. One of the main reasons I always see on applications is because people want more responsibility and while this may be true to an extent, you have to realize 98% of the applications I have seen in my career, have stated this. Make it interesting for the board and ensure you are truthful and be honest with the whole application, after all, you don't want to be the common amongst the applicants, you want to standout. I am probably one of the last Mustangs to have felonies in my background and that was one of my biggest selling points. My personal statement stated something to this affect "The guidance I received and chose not to listen to prior to joining the Navy compared to the difference of myself being guided by leaders in the U.S. Navy would have seemed the board was thinking we were talking about two separate people". So, you see that I really wanted to be honest and bring out what made me different from the other applicants. I brought the negative part of my application and made it into a positive, it may not work for everyone, but that is what I wanted to bring to the table and that is part of why I was selected. The reason I am going into so much detail at this moment, is there are a lot of competitive applicants, yet they do not sell themselves in the way they should. Remember, this is your commercial to the board to let everyone know why you must be selected. You have less than 400 words and you must be good during the short airtime that you get. So, if it is that you want to be financially set, you want to extend the possibility of staying in the Navy for another 14 to 24 years, or you were simply told you were never going to amount to anything, you have to express it correctly in the personal statement.

Should I wait for CPO?

With the understanding that some of the applicants for the LDO program are Chiefs who will be applying to become an LDO, and they have achieved an accomplishment which is the pinnacle of an enlisted career. I also have the understanding there are many who have moved up the ranks rather quickly and are thinking about applying for the LDO program. They only have one question in mind; should I wait to apply for Chief or should I apply immediately to become a Mustang. I am going to make this section very short and easy and I will start this off with this question. What is your end state goal? When you retire, do you want to be a Chief or do you want to retire as a Lieutenant, Lieutenant Commander, Commander, or even Captain. It is your choice? I can bring up many conversations up over the last 10 years, where approximately four or five personnel have advised me that they came upon this same question. They all chose to wait to become LDOs in exchange to carry the title of Chief. Some of these personnel were LDOs, some of them were Chiefs, one of them was a squared away Petty Officer First Class, one of them retired as a Commander and some of them could not apply for the

LDO program any longer because of the time in service requirement. They all waited to become Chiefs, except the Petty Officer who retired as an E-6, before applying for the LDO program. Guess what else they said, they would never have waited if they knew what the wait would have caused. The Commander had to retire due to high year tenure and the Chiefs retired as Chiefs. That's right, they all said they would not have waited. What does that mean for you? Go for the end state goal, don't wait for a title. The reason I bring this topic up in this book, is because I know this is an important topic in every LDO's career. Even for the Sailors who have accomplished this awesome feat of accomplishing the title of Chief, they themselves say should I stay in the mess or should I apply? Don't get me wrong, this is not a bashing at the mess, this is you looking out for yourself, your family and taking a deep look at where you best suit yourself for the Navy and our great country. I was stuck in this decision at the seven and a half year mark. I was never eligible to take the Chief exam for Chief advancement and only took the exam for LDO program purposes. Yes, selected on the first try, but this will not always be the case for everyone. So, yes, not a Chief, but the rest is history and I cannot guarantee that you will be selected on the first try, but remember what I brought up and that is "what is the end state goal"? Chief or LDO!

Why do I want this?

Don't ever think that once you are selected to become an LDO will it ever become easier for you in the Navy. At the same time, I am glad I went to a ship as a Head of Department on board an aircraft carrier than going onto a ship during my enlisted years. That I will not argue. Again, I state that once you place those butter bars on your collar or your pinstripe shoulder boards on, it will not become easier, although there will be certain privileges, which were not available to you prior to be commissioned. So why do you want to become an LDO? Why do you want to apply for this program? Why do you want the extra responsibility? The mention of these questions of why do you want to do this will have to be a question which you must find deep in the bottom of your heart and mind. Is it money or more responsibility? This might go back to the reasoning of why you joined the Navy. There might be certain situations which arose that you were not expecting in your lifetime, such as a divorce, a child support payment for the next 10-18 years, an extra family member who becomes a dependent and might be gravely ill, and the list continues. Maybe, you love your job and don't ever see yourself doing anything else in life, or you want to give the same aspirations to other Sailors, which you have at this moment. There are different reasons for everyone, but whatever the reasoning behind applying and wanting to be selected is your reasoning. The only person that can stop you from applying and the only one that can prevent you from being selected is yourself. Yes, there are certain items which will help you get selected, but if your goal is to really become an LDO, you will do everything in your honest power to become selected and no one will stop you. It's plain and simple why you want to be selected for this program. Only you will ever know the reason and not unless you sit down to think about why you are applying, you will never have the drive to be selected. Think about this reason and let it light up inside of you like a fire, don't ever let it run out!

Who motivated me to do this?

O ver the years, someone has motivated you to compete for this program. It might have been a family member when you were young, a Petty Officer in boot camp, maybe an LDO or a Chief at one of your previous commands, but someone sat you down somewhere along the way and prepped you up for this program. It could have been a simple action, gesture, speech, pep talk or even a retirement ceremony where you said, I want to do that or I can do that. Of course, it might not have been any of those and it was someone you approached for assistance and they recognized some characteristic in you as being worthy LDO material. No LDO makes it into the selection process without the assistance from an LDO; that one LDO who assists you, might have met you when you when you were a Seamen, others you might meet during the final stages of applying for the program. You just never know who that one Sailor, mentor or person will be and what exactly he/she will do to assist you, but no one does it by themselves. I always want to end these LDO topics of why do I bring these questions or subject up. This one is easy to explain, just as we all were assisted in being selected, we too, must help our reliefs. If selected, one day, someone will come up to you six months up to 20 years after you are selected to simply say, I want to become an LDO, can you look at my application. Don't ever forget where you came from as far too often I hear LDOs say they are too busy, don't have time, or there is this big inspection coming up at work. We all have those challenges, including the person who assisted you, and if it wasn't for that one person, you would not be selected. Enough said, don't forget where you came from!

Just because I want to put on khakis?

L et me get straight to the bottom of this section, don't simply apply to this program in the attempt to put on khakis. That is the worst type of mindset someone can have when applying for this program. Yes, it is a special achievement when someone gets the authority to put on khakis (even since the peanut butters came around), either as a commissioned officer or as a Chief, but to apply just to put on a specific uniform will only bring failure. It is with due time and hard work that you will be able to put on khakis, but to try to take a shortcut will not bring satisfaction. Why would I mention this or even think that someone is thinking like this? Simply said, someone has mentioned this exact statement to the author, stating they were tired of being denied for Chief, so they were going to apply for the LDO program. For the sake of the U.S. Navy, this individual was not selected to become an LDO, but in good part he was selected as a Chief Petty Officer in his 19th year of service and retired a year later. All he wanted was to wear khakis, I guess, putting on khakis was not for him, since he wore them less than a year. If this is what motivates a person to apply, then that is their right to apply, all that I am saying is, some Sailors will be disappointed when they are non-selected for a program they did not put all their heart into. Hard work and sustained superior performance is what will get you wearing khakis.

Am I ready to start?

This is a question you will have to ask yourself on the inner debate of when you are going to start your application along with the mindset that this is what you really want. Some applicants feel that being selected would be a nice to have challenge in their career and other applicants can't think of anything but being called Ensign (fill in your last name). If you are the second type of person why wait to apply. Remember what your goal is and that is to become a Mustang, not to remain as an enlisted and dwell in a certain rank. If you are waiting to advance to Chief or Senior Chief then maybe that is the route you should follow, but don't mislead people advising them that you are thinking about putting in an LDO application package before attaining the E-7 or E-8 rank. If you know that you are not going to do this, don't even bring it up. If you are happy where you are and don't want to go the officer route, there is nothing wrong with that. The Navy needs good Petty Officers and Chief Petty Officers, and leaders at all levels. There is nothing wrong with this and if anything, you have served your country with Honor, Courage, and Commitment. Here are a few examples of people in your life/career you might be saying this to, such as mentors, your LDO Division Officer or Department Head, superiors, peers, and even your spouse. Your spouse you should not be lying too and he/she is your equal other and there is no reason to lie to them. If anything, be honest about the situation and state why you don't want to apply. If they are really your equal, then they will understand, you might not make them happy, but they will understand. So, if you know you are ready, get that application and start hammering away at it. At the beginning the application may seem like a mountain, but by the time you submit it, in three months or five years, you will know the application like the back of your hand. The last subject in this section is procrastination, it is the killer of all goals and dreams, and sacrifice is how you overcome this goal killer. When people want to go out on the weekend, sacrifice! When you are just dead tired after a long day at work, sacrifice! You can't ignore your normal duty, and you can't ignore your family and everyone else all the time, but there are times, when you will have to prioritize your time with your family and determine how bad you want to submit this application and ensure your record is accurate. So, if you are ready, your application might not be the only item you need to sacrifice for, you might need that extra qualification, community hours, college, warfare, but you will have to sacrifice to make this goal a realization.

Who do I talk to?

Perfect question, who do you talk to, it all depends where you are at in your career and what command you are at. This is a tough question and although I cannot provide every answer, I can provide plenty of suggestions. You have to establish where you are in your career and how it relates to the LDO application process. Are you at your first command and have already started working on your application so when you pick up PO1, you submit one year after your time in rate? If you are still young in your career with three or more years before even submitting an application, start by getting an LDO mentor. Most LDOs love when a young, up and coming Sailor approaches them wanting guidance or assistance in the LDO program or another program. None-the-less, this is the major reason and usually the #1 statement listed on personal statements of why LDOs wanted to become an LDO. To inspire junior Sailors! Also, approach a Command Career Counselor (CCC) and attempt to get as much information as possible, they will not know it all, but they can steer you in the right direction. A lot of the times, LDOs approach CCC and ask if any Sailors are interested in the program. Lastly, if you are in a fleet concentration area such as

San Diego, Norfolk or any other Sailor saturated base, the chances are an LDO roadshow with detailers and senior LDOs show up such as community managers, detailers, meaning several LDOs will show up to talk to those detailers as well. By the end of the roadshow you will realize there may be close to 1,000 years of naval experience at that roadshow in just LDO experience. No, I am not over exaggerating with the years of experience. When detailers show up, so do LDOs, as they always want to know where they are going to next, even if they just arrived at their current command. As for the young Sailor attending a roadshow, this will feel uncomfortable, but if this program is what you really want, ensure you show up to be light years ahead of your competition when you eventually apply. Also, if you are blessed to attend one every year for three years in a row or longer, please do so as you will learn something new every time, or there might be changes in the program, which just occurred days before the roadshow arrived in your location.

Regardless if you are two years into the Navy or if you are 10 years into your career, always let your chain of command know that you are applying. From your LPO, Chiefs, and CMDCM and why you ask? There are two blocks in the back of your evaluation which state programs recommended for, those blocks should have a pattern in your evaluations every year from LDO program, commissioning program, maybe leadership recommendations such as Officer Candidate School, but those two little blocks should not be a surprise to anyone. Even though they are "programs recommended" everyone knows the chances are that the Sailor is the one who submitted the information on those blocks. If your chain of command does not believe you are officer material, remember that they have every right to change those blocks as they are recommended from your chain of command, not the Sailor. Just be aware those blocks exist!

If you are in a different scenario than the young Sailor I mentioned above and you will be applying soon within the next one to three years, you should have already have done everything I mentioned above. If you didn't, don't sweat the petty stuff, you are just going to have to put it into fifth gear and quickly! Additionally, besides having an LDO mentor at your command, you should also have one out of your command to bounce ideas off as well. It is not with the intent to suggest that two mentors are insufficient, but three heads are better than two and there is also the possibility that one LDO mentor may not have crossed a certain path and diversity of experience can only add to the learning process. While it is always good to have an LDO mentor in the designator you are applying for, it is not always necessary but it is helpful because they can assist you in designator specifics. Additionally, reach out to LDOs who may have been your DIVO, Department Head, or even Commanding Officer and the chances are, if you showed them you were LDO material before, they will only prep you up to welcome you to the Wardroom! So, start approaching LDOs, CCC, your supervisors and get on that Facebook LDO page to determine when that roadshow will be near you!

When should I start?

As mentioned in previous topics, I started working on my application when I was selected for MA2, which was on or about December 2002 and I did not even take the Chief exam for LDO purposes until January 2007 and officially submitted my application in October 2007. Some people would say that was foolish of me, others would say it was wise. I will say this, if I did not have those 100 revisions and several people looking at that package, I probably would not have been selected the first time. But since I was selected on the first go around, I would say those five plus years of working on the package was perfect for me. I did not give the board an opportunity to say no, with the well put together package and ensuring my record was up to par, the only answer the board could give me was "selected"!

I will say, the sooner you can start on your package the better. There is no right or wrong answer, it all depends on when you decide that being a Mustang is your end state goal! Some Sailors have had this goal from the minute they joined boot camp, maybe their father, mother, sister, brother were LDOs, maybe it was an influence of an LDO during boot camp or "A" school and from that moment on, they decided that is what they wanted to be. Other Sailors, may achieve Chief and realize that they only have two ranks to go before they are selected to their final rank and they only have been in eight years. They realize that if all goes well, they could possibly pick up Master Chief between their 14-18 year mark and now they are going to be a Master Chief for the next 12-16 years. Whatever the case when you decide that you want to apply, start the application as soon as possible, start asking the questions and start looking for those LDO mentors. We are out their waiting!

This is your package!

As I mentioned in the above previous topics, it is good to bounce this package with people you trust, LDO mentors, previous LDO supervisors and even civilians helped me out with inputs in writing the personal statement from a scholarly perspective. All this is good and dandy in order to make your package stronger, but the bottom line is, this is your package! Not your mentors, not your spouse's package and if you have an editor, not theirs either. There will be plenty of recommendations from people who have nothing but the best intentions for you, hear them out because they have possibly been members on previous boards, or they have looked at these packages for the past 10-22- years, but this is your package. I cannot make this any clearer, this package you have been putting together for months or even years is what you believe will get you selected. I have always believed that you will always learn from subordinates, peers, and superiors and some of these Sailors will provide lessons learned for the future, and some of these Sailors will teach you what not to do, and others will try to teach you certain items, which you may well be versed in, but that is how you have to treat your application. Listen to the inputs, adjust your application to the inputs that you think will help you get selected and throw out the inputs that add no value to your package. I have seen mentors get upset since you did not add certain items, or deleted certain items; what they need to understand is they are not you and you are not them. I am serious about this topic and I will finish this topic with the understanding that you must be tactful about how you approach the topic, as you yourself will be providing inputs in the future. There is no reason that anyone else should be upset about your application even if they think it will benefit you. Remember, when you have a solution at work, it may not be the same solution as your supervisors, but you still complete the job, it might be a different approach than how your supervisor would have completed the job. It doesn't make it wrong, it just makes the solution different and the same goes with your application. The end goal is to submit that application on time and to be selected!

Sell yourself like a commercial

What do I mean to sell yourself like a commercial? Your application is your commercial where you are selling your merchandise to the board and you are the merchandise! You are simply stating to the board on a few sheets of paper that you must be selected for LDO. Plenty of the sheets of paper are basic information such as your present command, social security number, projected rotation date, essentially, the same information you have filled out on paperwork at every command that you have checked into. So, what is the hard part about the application? Your personal statement for one, it is your 30 second message to the selection board why you want to be a commissioned officer, your goals and any other pertinent information you want the board to know. In other words, don't place on your personal statement all the positions you have held, awards which have been presented to you, or schools you have attended, as all these items are in your application. The selection board does not want to read the same items which are in the previous pages. They want to know exactly why you are applying and what differentiates you from the rest of the pack. As mentioned several times, you will be going up against First

Class Petty Officers through Senior Chief Petty Officers, so why are you the one? Also, take into consideration depending on your designator, some designators will select 25 new accessions, while others might only select six, so that is another factor. None-the-less, you have to explain yourself in your personal statement that you are worthy of selection. It could be that you were a juvenile delinquent and the Navy set you straight, or you want to be financially stable with more pay, maybe throughout your career other Sailors have told you that you would never be a commissioned officer. Maybe your father and grandfather were Mustangs and you want to continue the tradition in the family, whatever the situation is, explain to the board in 400 simple words.

The other portion of the application where you really must sell is based on your Commanding Officer's recommendation, so this should have the personal touch from the Commanding Officer. You might have come out with a template, or a draft format, but your Commanding Officer must show on the recommendation he is really trying to sell you to the board. Not the same old stuff as "SELECT THIS SAILOR NOW!" It should show that he really did some background work on your record and that he collaborates your personal statement with goals, purpose and any other pertinent information. I had an O-10 write on the application that if any questions arise, to give him a call at his personal cell phone, which blew me out of the water! It was great to see that from him, and not only did it mean a lot to me, imagine what the board members thought.

Lastly, the extracurricular activities section of the application comes from what you have done, such as community service, coaching little league baseball, even certifying Sailors as scuba divers, but you have to show the cause and effect of the extracurricular activity. I have seen some applications, where they stated "1) I like to fish, 2) I like to run.......... you get the idea. These well thought out activities such as "Member volunteered 45 hours to the Smithville soup line which served 1,500 meals to homeless citizens, and helped decrease crime in the city by 15%. This may be extreme, but ensure each activity shows cause and effect. You did some activity, and in return because off of your activity, there was a positive in return. Only you know what you have done, what you want to do, and what your purpose in obtaining a commission is, so in the best way possible advertise yourself in order to be selected.

Is my family ready?

Without a doubt, I have to make a section for the family members and spouses, at least just a brief one. As mentioned in previous chapters, if you don't have the support of your spouse and kids, you will never be successful, both inside or outside the Navy. You as well have to be committed to them in order to be in sync to achieve the same goals. I have never met a spouse who stated he/she was not happy their spouse was selected for LDO. If anything, the spouse is usually as excited as the military member or even more excited knowing that the family provided the support to the military member and contributed to the selection of becoming an LDO. Very seldom, do you find an LDO who states that he/she were selected without any assistance from his family. When the selection message comes out in February or March of every year welcoming new Mustangs to the wardroom, I advise the spouses that the sacrificing and the support is just about to start. The look I get from some of the spouses with jaws dropping, they believed that the Navy was going to get easier. If anything, the time at the office will be consumed with what the military member places on the personal statement section. Yes, many LDOs stated on their personal statement they wanted to make changes in the Navy, implement policies which were going to affect their rate, start programs and the list goes on, well this is what is going to prolong the hours at work. Remember, the Navy does not give money away for free, I have never encountered a situation where money is provided for doing nothing and in this case the LDOs who were selected was for the purpose of the U.S. Navy getting something in return for the raises that they are providing to the new accession LDOs. Some Sailors are getting anywhere from $500 to $1,000 pay raise, two years later they will receive another $1,000 and two years after that they will be receiving another $1,000. The intent of giving someone these pay raises is that they will be producing results. But, as the work progresses, so does the paycheck and the lifestyle. You enjoy the paycheck with items you have always wanted, vacations, bigger budgets, etc. and although money is not my first priority, money does make life easier. So, while I say that it will not be all roses as a commissioned officer, I will say that the military member will still continue to need the support of the spouse and the family. While you will continue to sacrifice and support the military member, enjoy the lifestyle!

Am I even competitive?

Only one person knows if you are competitive and that is yourself, you have to be honest with yourself. At a recent LDO interview board, I mentioned to a Chief that if he really wants to become an LDO, he needs to be all in with the program. I further advised him, he should not apply just to see what the possibilities will be on selection results. You as the applicant, need to confirm that this is what you really want. While there are several LDOs who apply at the last minute, chances are they had probably been thinking about applying for several years, meaning they have worked hard over the course of their career. As mentioned in the previous topic "What will help me?" You know deep down inside how hard you have worked for this program based on the requirements the selection board looks for. You are also aware if you are competitive, and as I mentioned to that Chief, you really have to strive to be selected. If you are second guessing yourself on how competitive you are, you are probably not 100% immersed in this program. Please don't be confused with a little fear and not knowing if you are competitive. Everyone experiences both trepidation and excitement waiting for the selection results just like any promotion, but if you are wondering if you should apply, you have not placed 100% effort into really wanting this program.

I am a FCPO and I might be going up against SCPO

This is the eye opener statement I always bring up to First Class Petty Officers during the interviews. "You are a First Class Petty Officer who will be competing against Chiefs and Senior Chief Petty Officers". If you are in this situation, what will make you outshine your competition? Think about this, you are an E-6 who will be competing against a khaki who is only one rank away from reaching the highest rank of the enlisted ranks and you want to compete against them. Now that I have worked this topic up to a suspense, please understand that selection is not about the rank, but about your achievements and sustained superior performance. Year in and year out, I have heard from many Chiefs who stated they did not get selected, but I am also aware of several First Class Petty Officers who were selected for those designators during the same fiscal year. Many personnel assume Chiefs have a higher probability of being selected than a First Class Petty Officer. While I do not know if this is true, your application can compete. Selection, on the other hand, will depend on how good an application you submit.

At one time, I had the same fear I would not be able to compete against the Chiefs and my chain of command had also ranked me #3 of #3 applicants; it was explained to me that a Chief had to be placed at a higher ranking than a First Class Petty Officer. When the selection board met, they saw right through the rankings and only I was selected out of the three personnel that applied from my command. This proves that the rank of the applicant is not an advantage or the only deciding factor on the selection process.

Selected

Congratulations, you just saw the "S" on your BUPERS online account and you are now selected to be a Mustang. You don't care if your commissioning month is October of the fiscal year you applied or 11 months later in September of the fiscal year you applied, you are selected and you are on cloud 9. There is no better feeling than the first day you are formally notified, just ensure you enjoy this first day. I still remember the tension leading up to the day I was selected, traveling in a German airport while heading to a mission in Ghana with one of my shipmates and my best friend. I assumed I was being a pain as the stress piled on knowing results would be out soon. But once the results were released, all this stress was released as well and I was filled with a happiness which could not be avoided. I never felt so much joy in my Navy career associated with a certain accomplishment (and you will too) simply for the reason that this was the goal I had set approximately five years before. All praise to God! Ensure you enjoy this time with the people that supported you as they too should be celebrating this moment with you. If you knew this was going to happen you have already inquired about Mustang University, uniforms, pay, commissioning ceremony, orders, and everything that comes with the upcoming promotion. So, continue to enjoy the selection and continue prepping up for the future.

Now what?

〜〜〜

Okay, a couple of days to several weeks have passed since the official notification that you will soon become a Mustang, but what do you do now? As mentioned toward the end of the last topic, you have a lot to inquire about, especially if you had not done any homework on your future. Let's start off with your enlisted career, don't stop what you are doing and continue to be a hard charger, this is what helped you get selected, but there are certain items you must understand. You are now in a selected status for evaluations, it does not matter if you are a First Class Petty Officer or a Chief Petty Officer. Your evaluations will not affect your commission, nor your promotion to Lieutenant Junior Grade, unless, you give up and tarnish everything you have worked for and you are prevented from being commissioned. You are not trying to promote to the next rank and not unless you are from a major command such as an aircraft carrier, the chances of another LDO being selected from your command are slim, possible, but slim. Why do I mention this? Time to let your collateral duties go, do a proper turnover as per your chain of command and ensure other Sailors receive the same opportunity you did with the collateral duties. Second, if you are in a leadership position, talk to your chain of command about giving another Chief or fellow First Class Petty Officer an opportunity at a leadership position. Please don't take this the wrong way and start trying to tell your chain of command what to do. Be tactful and responsible about the whole situation, as you still have superiors; you are not an Ensign yet and even then, you will have superiors. There will be timelines to start letting go of certain duties, but don't go into your Division Officer's office the day after you are notified of the selection and say you are not going to work again until the day of your commissioning. Guess what, you may be the only Chief in the division or no one else is ready to step up to the plate and you might have to wait until you are commissioned. Don't misunderstand, the duties and responsibilities will go away, although some might take longer than others. You must also prep up other Sailors for their future, guide them and provide recommendations to assist them in their careers. You will see how Sailors will start reacting to your guidance, some will listen and others will test you. Lastly, you have plenty to think about and to do in the near future to include ceremonies and uniforms, but you can't do this alone. Please reach out to an LDO who can assist you with your questions, ceremonies, and challenges you may be encountering. You need an LDO mentor to help out with the process, not to mention your permanent change of station, travel, travel pay, commissioning paperwork and the list continues. One last thing, you are either an Ensign, Senior Chief, Chief, or First Class, but you are not an Ensign select. There is no such thing and you should never introduce yourself with that title. I understand you are happy, joyful, even prideful that you were selected, but some of you might be in a selected status for up to 18 months, which is a long time to be stating a false rank, please don't embarrass yourself. There is much to do during this waiting game, one thing not to do is place a negative spotlight on yourself. In the next topic, let's talk about a fun item: detailers.

Detailers

For me, this was the best part of the selection as now you get to possibly move to a new location. That's right, moving for me is always the best part of the military, you get to enjoy a new location, new cultures, new command, new people and new shipmates. This is not even mentioning what your family gets to enjoy as well with new houses, new schools, friends and adventures. Remember, now that you are selected, prepare for where the Navy needs you, chances are this is what you wrote on your personal statement. I understand some people have the intention of homesteading in certain fleet concentration areas, which at times, detailers will try to work with the Officer and with the billets they have. Yet, not everyone can always be offered what they want and as all good leaders know, there are Sailors to be led in other areas of the world besides Norfolk, San Diego, Bremerton and Jacksonville/Mayport. The reasoning I bring this up is I always hear or see LDOs who are happy that they were able to get one maybe two tours in a fleet concentration area, yet are extremely upset when they are advised to go overseas or a different fleet concentration area. You can't always expect to stay in the same location for the next 10 to 20 years, so please be prepared and don't be upset if you are not offered your first request. Also, you shouldn't expect as a Lieutenant Commander to take an Ensign billet in order to stay in the same location and I would not expect detailers to allow this to happen as well. So, what should you expect when calling the detailer once you are selected? Be prepared to explain what you want out of the first tour of your commissioned career, your goals, warfare qualification, career enhancing additional qualification designations, locality, possible personal challenges such as your children's school year, exceptional family member program, etc. Your commissioning month has plenty to do with the detailer's priority based on fairness and situations which could arise. An example of this fairness would be that a detailer will first want to talk to a new accession LDO who is getting commissioned in October of the fiscal year than a new accession LDO who is getting commissioned 11 months later. Why? A lot can happen in a matter of months where a person may not be able to fill a certain billet, such as a certain billet at a command becomes obsolete, personal challenges arise such as a death in the family or a family member is not able to accompany the Sailor due to an exceptional family member. Be prepared for what the Navy offers, it may not always be what you want, yet at times you may be offered your dream job.

Have you met your goal; are you done?

You are selected and you have been waiting patiently. But now is the time to start thinking about what you really want in your career! You have the next 10 to possibly 30 years of Navy life ahead of you, what do you really want now that you have been selected. There are many career goals, both professional and personal which you might be looking into. So, what are they? That is for you to sit down with your mentor and see what your intentions are and don't forget to sit down with your spouse and family to include them. This will impact all family members from moving every two to three years to even traveling overseas, the increase in pay and what you will invest the extra pay in. The chances of not being able to homestead in a fleet concentration area any longer could impact your family, especially if your kids are young and will be required to attend different schools. The understanding that you will need to save a few thousand dollars for uniforms, travel, and whatever else required for a move. You don't want to be that person, who shows up with one pair of khakis and doesn't go out to eat because of poor planning, high amount of debt and irresponsibility. Your purpose for becoming an LDO is to give other Sailors the same aspirations you had in becoming an LDO. One of the goals you should be passing on is to not be worrying about bills, because you live beyond your means. When you are promoted, the last item you should be worrying about is to continue living beyond your means, you should be thinking about how you are going to invest. Believe me, it feels better when the interest rates are in your favor. Give Sailors positive advice which will contribute to them reaching their goals. This mentor I mentioned at the beginning of the topic is the one you have to rely on to assist you with your goals for your designator and the current rate you are in and guess who else is one of your mentors? Like it or not, your detailers will be giving you advice for the better part of your careers. I have been blessed to have good detailers and ones that understand. Figure out what you want to do, but now is not the time to start thinking about retirement as you are the one who is starting your commissioning career.

Waiting, the real hard part!

Okay, so you are selected, now what? Everything you have ever wanted and everything you had ever worked for is here NOW! Congratulations, now hurry up and wait. I am not teasing, but I know exactly what you are feeling at this moment. You have never been so excited to promote to the next rank, but you have usually waited anywhere from a week for frocking to one of the Petty Officer ranks or, worse case scenario, you had to wait approximately six weeks to pin on those anchors. Well, in this case, you will have to wait as little as eight months to as much as 19 months. Wow, what a wait, but believe me, it is well worth it. You just have to be patient and continue working with the same work ethics that helped you get selected. You just have to understand that people will be looking at you in a different way, even though you are not wearing those bars yet, people will start acting like you are. Some personnel will look at you as if you are their boss already, others will drag this long wait hoping that you will never be their boss. These acts will come out of fear, some will come out of joy from true shipmates, and others will show you what true hate is. You will have to be humble, understand that not everyone is happy that you were selected and that is a known fact. It is not a good feeling, but these are feelings you will have to live through and will only build character. This will assist you in the future during this long wait in understanding how people think, how they work, and how you will lead.

So, what can you do while you wait? There is plenty you can do, as there is plenty you can still learn. Remember, just because you were selected does not mean that you know everything, it just means that you were one of the better personnel who applied the year you were selected and that the board believed you would succeed as an LDO. So, if you talked to your detailer and know where you are going for your first commissioned tour, then you will have a step ahead of the game in learning your upcoming duties and or position. If you know your next location, contact the person you are relieving or your sponsor and attempt to obtain standard operating procedures, instructions or just read up on the position you will be filling through OPNAV instructions, which will only prepare you for the future. If you think you are going to show up with the shiny butter bars at your first command as if you are Superman, you have another thing coming. Those butter bars will not solve everything, if anything they will solve nothing, it will be your mind, your leadership skills and the way you communicate with people, which will be necessary and required. So, prepare yourself, especially if you are heading to a command, which you have never worked in a similar position before.

Lastly, I give you guidance to continue working and assisting the command that helped you get selected. Some of you might be put into a leadership position in order to groom you for similar, future positions, others might be moved out of their current position in order to be placed in a special projects position, so you can assist your department or your command until you transfer. Whatever predicament you are placed in, ensure you do homework and the job is done correctly. Remember, you were just selected to be a Mustang, a Naval Commissioned Officer, so you can lead people, change programs and complete the mission. You need to be ready and don't think someone will be waiting to prep you up to be a great LDO at your first command. As some Mustangs have come to realize, they will show up at their first command with the intentions of being a Division Officer, and arrive realizing the Department Head was relieved, not fit for sea duty and congratulations you are now the Department Head. You never know what to expect on day one, you might receive some on-the-job training on day one, you might not, so ensure you brush your skills up as much as possible prior to arriving and while you are waiting.

People will want to bring you down!

How can I say this without hurting anyone's feelings? People will be jealous, upset, and will do everything in their power to bring you down until you fail. Some people, but not all! Some of them are upset because they were not selected while others will be upset because they did not apply. So, who are these people? They could be peers, subordinates, heck even superiors that did not think you were worthy of the accolade. I will try not to prolong this topic, just be aware and the best advice I can give you, is to work until the end of your tour. Not one day short! Be respectful, tactful, and always remember this promotion of you being selected to be a Mustang is a blessing. Don't waste the blessing and ensure you show people that you have earned this promotion. If you still feel the hate, continue on and overcome this obstacle. Don't think for a second that once you put those butter bars on, that this type of attitude towards you goes away. There will always be people who want to challenge you, think they are smarter than you, or simply attempt to prove you wrong. Overcome with a smile and get it done!

What/Who do you want
in the ceremony?

All right, time is getting closer and you have now relinquished plenty of your duties, responsibilities, and collateral duty positions. This will be a special day in your life, so don't be foolish as I was and ignore the ceremony. That's right, my mindset as a young Sailor was that I was going to be promoted another five times after this so this milestone in my career should not be overexaggerated. You never know what will happen while you are in uniform and that is the unknown, so enjoy every milestone you are about to accomplish. I was part of a component commander staff, so I wanted a four-star to swear me in to the ward room in a small conference room. My family had moved back to the states to prep up for the new school year, so I figured this was a good enough ceremony. I mean, how many of us have been sworn into the ward room by an O-10, there are some, but not many! Once the Admiral heard this, he advised the bull Ensign (another LDO) to make a small gathering. Which turned out to be a great ceremony! Thank you for taking care of me. With this I say, the first step in making sure your ceremony is ready to go, ensure you get some assistance. You will need a mentor to assist and ensure you are correct with the programming and 50/60. Yes, it is smart to not rewrite the book, but you will have to conduct plenty of work on that 50/60, because no two ceremonies are the same. This is where the mentor comes in to give you pointers, ideas in which he/she may have seen in previous ceremonies. Take the ideas, as it never hurts to listen to, even if you do not use them for your ceremony. Next, ensure you receive assistance from a peer, shipmate, or maybe even someone who is going to be commissioned a couple of months behind you as this will help them gain the experience needed for their ceremonies.

Lastly, very similar to your LDO application, this is your ceremony, not your mentors, not your peers, but yours, so make it as such. Prep up as much as possible leading up to the ceremony, by saving as much money for the ceremony. I made mine to be very inexpensive and the Mustang Association pitched in for the majority of it and the Admiral pitched in for the food. Yet, I have seen some new accession fly-in family members in abundance, somewhere between 10-20 family members paid by the new accession. I am not suggesting you to do this, but I understand how important family is and you may already have the funds to do this, although chances are you will have to save. How much? This is up to the new accession, but this is your ceremony, so there is no right or wrong answer, no such thing as spending too little or too much, but this is a personal choice, not a requirement.

USAA Low interest loan

Why would I be mentioning this topic in this book, because no one ever mentioned this to me while I was going through the process after I was selected. I don't know how much longer this loan will continue, but it was a great opportunity for my family and me to start off from a clean slate involving our financial state. I will be the first one to state that I was not in the best financial position when I was commissioned, but I will say that within one year of being commissioned, we were debt free. There was no better feeling than to be debt free and finally having a decent paycheck every two weeks, meaning I would be able to start investing some money. How did this happen? USAA has a low-interest loan, which will assist newly commissioned officers in the Navy. All you have to do is call USAA and advise them that you were recently commissioned in the U.S. Navy and they will loan you up to $25,000 for a low rate. If you do not require the loan, ignore this section and continue on to the next. I would rather have you financially stable than to have you take out a loan just because you can. In all honesty, this is the last case scenario and goes against my current beliefs on taking out loans. It is just a perk, but not a requirement.

Financially stable

This is a requirement and not just a perk, that's right you need to stay financially stable and if you are not there, you need to get there as soon as possible. Why you ask? I want you to learn and listen to people who have learned and I want you to learn from my mistakes. How do you stay financially stable in this career? I will ask you how do you not stay financially stable? You are getting an approximate pay raise of $500 to $1,000 a month, so how do you get out of debt? Two simple rules, don't live beyond your means and stay away from credit (debt) and credit cards (debt cards). Yes, simple rules, but no one wants to listen to these simple rules. How hard is it to live below your means? Well, for over half of America, it is extremely hard. People tend to believe they will always need to have a car payment for the rest of their lives, that everyone always needs a credit card and now you have a good paycheck, so you definitely need to have a bigger car, more items, and even possibly a bigger house. Wrong! Why don't you invest that money, but first you must get rid of debt, those car payments and even the house payments. You see, there is a supposition you must have all these items, but in actuality, you need to understand that most people acquire these items through debt and not liquid funds. It happens in all ranks from blue shirts, to Chief's Mess, and we are no better, it happens in the ward room. Pretty ridiculous if you ask me, everyone trying to keep up with the Jones'. Too bad everyone knows, the Jones' are broke, living off of credit cards and debt. Don't be them! This really hits close to home, because no ever taught me this, not the Navy, not a financial counselor, no one except my sister-in-law who gave me some advice to get rid of debt. It was all basic information, which I already knew, yet I never took the steps into action. Why? Simply because I was unintentionally trying to keep up with the Jones' and living beyond my means with the plastic. Now that you have some extra cash rolling into the bank account, begin and finish these financial steps and stick to them, it is not impossible, just a harder road to follow. Start up an emergency fund, pay off all debt, grow that emergency fund to three to six months of your pay (return and refill this emergency fund if ever used), increase your Thrift Savings Plan (TSP) to anywhere from 10 to 20%, start investing with the guaranteed rank promotions you will be receiving in the next two to four years. That's right, you will be receiving between $1,000 to $2,200 per month in the next two to four years. Just because you receive more money, does not mean you need to spend more money. So, after you follow all these steps, invest with a goal, don't just put money in an account. Save with a meaning, with a goal, with a purpose. Look, there are several people that provide good financial living advice for you such as your financial advisors, Dave Ramsey, Chris Hogan and the list continues on. I like these two because they are honest, God fearing men. This promotion is a blessing, take advantage and don't waste it like some have done.

Retire with Class not with Debt

So, you have 12 to 30 years left in the military and you can save quite a bit during this time frame, especially with all the pay raises which are bound to occur. You can save anywhere from $200,000 plus to close to a million dollars, if you can put away $2,000 a month for the remainder of your career not to mention the compound interest you will obtain and the TSP you have been putting away since you were an E-1. Let me add this to the equation, you will also be receiving a pension for the rest of your life, a good one I may add. While you should not solely depend on your pension, it is hard to ignore that you will receive a pension. God willing, all goes well and you don't die the minute you retire. But let's assume you will live a long time. This is exactly how you want to retire, but if you are not responsible with your finances throughout your career, there is a possibility this is not how you will start your retirement. How can this be a bad retirement? Let's add to the mix a divorce with alimony (to include 50% of our pension), child support times two for the next 16 years, a maxed out $20,000 credit card, two payments for luxury cars, and a house with a $3,000 a month mortgage payment for the next 27 years. While it will not be impossible to get out of this situation, it will be difficult. You must realize that your intentions are to retire and not to stay working in order pay off debt and situations you chose, which will not place you in the best predicament if all these are factors. No mistakes, just consequences, some good, some bad.

Mustang U

Mustang University is also known as Knife and Fork school. You are officially in Newport, Rhode Island the state you never expected to be in when you joined the military unless you were going to be a submariner. But you are here and you are ready to take over the world as you are now on your first official command where you will be wearing those bars. What a feeling and now you are showing up to be with the best of the best Sailors, nothing but your fellow LDO Mustangs in the famous Knife and Fork school you have been hearing about for the last few months to the last couple of years. Some of you have been wearing khakis for a few years, other were First Class Petty Officers and now you are wearing them as well, but one thing you have to take into consideration is that no one wore those bars except for the past couple of days to the last few weeks. Chances are the minute you were commissioned, you started your PCS, so you never really able to wear the bars or the uniform. Meaning, everyone there is in the same position. This is the mindset you must have when you attend Mustang U. Everyone is the same when you get there and when you leave. With the exception of the lineal numbers which you will get in the future, every one of you who attend are commissioned on the same date of the same month. Should there be any uneasiness when you arrive and attend Mustang U? No, you shouldn't, but for whatever reason we all do. While attending Mustang U, please listen to me and understand that networking is a must and will help you in the future, especially fellow LDOs from your designator. Please understand that almost every single LDO who attends Mustang U is probably an Alpha type male/female and they did not get where they are, because they are used to somebody telling them what to do. They all want to be bosses and that is the feeling of uneasiness, which follows everyone into these four to five weeks, regardless of what your rank was prior to being commissioned. On the first day of course, everyone is walking around with their guard up and ready to attack; awkward but true. Additionally, deep down inside everyone is happy, they are there with the best of the best and you have all type of backgrounds at this location. The one item everyone is looking at on everyone else is the "chest candy". That's right, they want to see what awards you have, how many deployments you have, if you have deployed to war zones, seen combat, you name it, everything that can be displayed on your chest is what they are looking to see. Along with this test, your peers are looking to see if you were a Chief, Senior Chief or a First Class, its classic, but there is no way they can tell, unless they ask and I am not making this up. I tell you this to prepare you and to let you understand that the playing field is the same. It just depends on your designator and how every rate is different. I walked into Knife and Fork school with a Joint Commendation Medal, Navy / Marine Corps Commendation Medal and three Navy / Marine Corps

Achievement Medals, so people assumed I was not a First Class Petty Officer when I was commissioned, but as soon as they asked I told them the truth with pride, after all, why lie? There were Chiefs and Senior Chiefs who walked in there with two Navy / Marine Corps Achievement Medals and had a division of 15 Sailors. Do you see where I am going with this? You were selected for a reason and once selected, different leaders receive different lessons learned, some find this experience at a young time in service, while others don't get this type of experience until 15 to 20 years in, it all depends. Don't assume because you were of a certain rank, you automatically know more. To follow this conversation, your next duty station, which will be the first one as an Officer, will say a lot about you as well. I was going to be an Ensign with close to 10 years in service and I was selected to be a Department Head, wow, what a rush! Right next to me were Ensigns who were prior Senior Chiefs that were headed to be a Division Officer on a carrier. This really goes back to the statement of "choose your rate, choose your fate". You do learn a lot from each other and if you go in with an open mind, you can really take an abundance of information with you, some of this information will help you out in the future, but a lot of Mustang U consists of personnel telling sea stories and exchanging information which will help each other out. I will never take anything away from that school, even when we had to march as if we were in boot camp all over again, it was perfect. Why? Because I was now a Mustang and no one should believe that simply because you are now commissioned the Navy was going to become a perfect place for you to work. Don't get me wrong, it is definitely the greatest Navy in the world, in all of history and you are a part of it. You can now say you are a commissioned Naval Officer in the greatest Navy in the world. What did I learn at Knife and Fork school? The do's and don'ts of being a commissioned officer, what will get you fired and what you have to do to continue being successful in the U.S. Navy. In the first day of class, back in 2009, we were advised where to sit with nametags on the chairs. Nothing out of the ordinary and all of a sudden, an old salty LCDR with a big red mustache shows up and introduces himself as our primary instructor. He mentioned that one of our fellow LDOs who was commissioned the same month we were had died a couple of days prior to reporting to Mustang U due to a motorcycle accident in San Diego, CA. It was some way to start off the class but the next couple of items was where he really gave us some advice that, as an LDO, you need to carry with you for the rest of your career. As we were in shock about the loss of our shipmate, the instructors had posted the news article and his picture in the back of the room. He advised us to go back there and see if any of us knew him, which one or two people stated they were aware of his death. It was disheartening and a reality check, that we can be gone from one day to the next. We must ensure we don't sell our careers short out of fear of dying, but I wanted to bring this story in remembrance of this shipmate that I never met, but meant a lot to me. The instructor told us to sit down and then explained a few items and then starts asking questions, which I will never forget. First, he asks to raise our hands if any of us were Sailor of Year at previous commands and, as I shrink down in my chair, everyone else raises their hands. EVERYONE! Boy, did I feel small, I think to myself, do I belong here? Everyone puts their hands down, a few giggles here and there. I don't know if they were directed at me or not, but I always felt that they were laughing at me. The next question did not get much better, he asked how many of you were Chiefs prior to being commissioned? There I go again, melting in my chair and with the exception of five people to include myself, all the LDOs raised their hands. He tells everyone to put their hands down and again I hear the giggles and sly comments. I was wondering when he was going to stop with these nonsense questions as I felt humiliated and angered at this point. I wanted to go away and never come back. I always felt inferior amongst superiors, but this was one of the few times in my career where I felt inferior around my peers. Not normal! He ended the barrage of questions with this statement. Those of you who were Sailor of the Year at a certain command and Chiefs or higher, go put that stuff in your "I love me binders" because none of that means anything while you are wearing these bars. Man, did I feel relieved. Next, he goes into the number one rule of what not to do as an LDO and that is not to mess with the help, in other words, don't have affairs/relationships and/or fraternize with junior Sailors. He gives several sea stories about shipmates of his hooking up with E-3's who looked like models and were 15 years younger. He mentioned this was a common occurrence in the fleet and to just stay away from it and if you are aware of the situation, report it as soon as possible, because you could be lured into the mess if you keep it to yourself. Finally, he asked some questions, which indicates what items we can cross over from our enlisted career to our officer careers. These are very important and great information to know as you can prep for this as a junior enlisted Sailor understanding you can cross the following information over. His question was, what three items can crossover from the enlisted ranks to the officer ranks. After several answers which were not what he was expecting, he tells us. All the LDOs were thinking about experience, maturity and lessons learned, which were correct, but were not the answers he was looking for. He asked how many of us have an Associate Degree, so I raise my hand and I like where this is going. I may not be the smartest person in any room, but I am an educated person, praise God! You wouldn't expect it out of me because I am brown, of Mexican descent, but people don't realize I am one of the other Mexicans, who is fourth generation American. I can say with the exception of two to five people, everyone raised their hands. He continues on and asked how many of us had a Bachelor Degree and I keep my hand raised. Half of the class puts their hands down and he asked how many of us have a Master Degree or higher? Only two of us keep our hands up and with pride. He asked if we were planning to continue on with our PhD? I mentioned I was enrolled in a PhD program and the instructor and the rest of the class looked at me, like if I was crazy. He made me feel like I belonged now and he states, that sheep skin on the wall is one of the few items you can carry over from the enlisted ranks. He further states that these two gentlemen with a Master Degree will be the competition in the future and that they already have a step ahead for the O4 board, which means the others had 10 years to catch up. The second item he mentioned, is your chest candy to include your warfare insignias. He went into the questions of who has what awards to include Navy / Marine Corps Achievement and Commendation Medals, Individual Joint awards, Bronze Stars and I felt I was pretty competitive with this section as well. I think about his questions now and I believe his purpose was to level the playing field and have people understand why they were selected to become an LDO. While some individuals were selected for certain reasons and others for different reasons, we all have something to give to the ward room. The remainder of Mustang U was networking, physical training and learning basic Officer items, which we might have already known, but were great refresher items. One thing I will close this topic out with is because of his questions, we all knew we belonged in the LDO community and regardless of who was educated, who was a prior Chief, we all respected each other. Oh yeah, what was that third item? Your skills you obtained as an enlisted Sailor! Next stop, the fleet.

Superman/Superwoman with those butter bars and prepping for that first day of work

The first day of work is here and the Navy has given you training in abundance, sent you to school after school to obtain qualifications, earn NECs, and here you are with your butter bars ready to conquer. After all, the Navy has awarded you with a promotion that most Sailors don't receive and you are also a different type of commissioned officer who was prior enlisted. You will be bringing a different type of experience to the ward room and everyone is going to respect you because you are an officer, an LDO at that. This will be a difficult experience and one not to be taken lightly as you will have respect as an LDO Mustang, but just as at every command you have ever checked into, you will have to show your worthiness. You are continuing your Naval career at a higher rank, but when you check into a command, do you automatically receive an early promotion and not have to show your work ethic and your drive to get the mission complete? Negative, you are tested day in and day out, along with having to take care of your subordinates, peers, and superiors. So, don't expect anything different on this first day of work. People are excited to know who you are, they are wanting to see if you are going to make a difference and if you are going to have an effect on their division or department. What a rush, you have received some type of pass-down from the person you are relieving, but it is always different when you get there. No matter what you were advised there will always be changes. I am telling you this out of experience, and every command that has followed has continued to be the same. At my most recent command, which is my fourth commissioning tour, I was advised that it is laid back, no travel will occur and be prepared to enjoy the Rota, Spain sunrays. Upon checking in to my command, it cannot be laid back, because it is an operational command, I have traveled almost every month to include 30 days or more TAD stints and have not been able to enjoy much of the Rota sunrays as advised. Am I complaining? No, I am just telling you so you can understand and you can let your spouse know that there will always be changes. Additionally, while these changes occur, one item I remind everyone, no complaining. You were blessed with a great opportunity, not to complain, but to overcome. Remember, you are a Mustang, you plug holes and fix issues, not complain about them. Plus, you don't want your junior personnel complaining all the time as well.

Okay, so you check in and you will encounter lessons learned over the next few years and these lessons will continue to help you for the remainder of your career. These same lessons and challenges will be asked on LDO boards and were probably asked to you as well. 99% of the questions asked on boards are from factual incidents which have occurred in the paths of LDOs. The ironic situation about these lessons learned is when I am about to ask a question from an incident that has occurred in my career, another LDO on the board asks the same question meaning these lessons learned happen on more than one occasion. So, don't be surprised if you are planning to show up to be the assistant department head or a division officer and you are advised you are going to take over two divisions or an entire department. You will have to overcome and there is no overtime pay. You might be the prior First Class Petty Officer who takes over Training Department and the Weapons Division simultaneously and has two Master Chiefs, three Senior Chiefs, four Chiefs awaiting guidance from the new Ensign. Wow, what a rush; but a true story.

A long-standing situation in the Navy is when a prior-enlisted LDO reports to your command, they will become either one of the ones you look up to or one of the most hated officers in your wardroom. My own observations support this, and I think that I have personally been on both sides of this topic at times. As mentioned, LDOs come with unique perspectives and experiences that can benefit the command, but if the prior-enlisted identity is mismanaged it can dominate the individual, decreasing their growth and creating divisions within the ranks.

Which side of the "Good Prior/Bad Prior" challenge one falls is not a factor of their personality; it's really an attribute of how they deal with situations and how they were brought up in the Navy. An LDO who falls on the bad part of the spectrum can be corrected. From what I've seen, enlisted commissioning programs do little to address the unique challenges which come with the transition to the ward room. If you were to walk into any wardroom today and ask someone to describe an LDO they dislike, you'd probably get the same description wherever you went. This LDO described refuses to transition, identifying more strongly with the mess or the First Classes and he/she draws attention to himself. Additionally, this LDO seeks any opportunity they can to differentiate from the other ensigns, whether it's by bringing their experience into the conversation, brandishing that they are a Mustang, or creating a reputation of salty, abrasive attitude, which really causes a bad name for us all. They will do the bare minimum necessary to get them to the next rank or to retirement and they brag about this. Meanwhile, they consistently talk about how hard they have worked to get where they are as an LDO, implying that other officers who have gone through different commissioning programs did not. This is why I dislike the statement LDOs state and wear on their paraphernalia "we did it the hard way, we earned it". So, the Naval Academy graduate or the ROTC officer did not because they were commissioned the traditional way. Wrong, we all have earned this commission. While it may be hard to go from the top of the enlisted ranks to the bottom of the commissioning ranks, this is a rank you have earned and if you applied for this program, you were aware of going from the top to the bottom, so don't act like if someone owes you something. No one likes these type of LDOs who walk around cursing at people, being a bully, it doesn't get you anything at all. If you see your fellow LDOs or other Sailors acting like this, react quickly and nip this in the butt.

To finish this topic, always remember to be humble and you did not get to this rank based on one day, one action, or one merit, so you will not have all the answers on the first day you show up. You decide when you stop obtaining the information you need to lead and, along with not having all the answers, you need to know where to get these answers. Lastly, the Navy is an ever-evolving agency, new instructions, new directives, and new programs, which means you must keep up with new items as well. Don't stop learning and there is someone out there always hungrier than you are. Which type of LDO are you going to be? Just don't be the one nobody likes.

Prepping for the rest of your career

Staying competitive throughout your career is next on the list. The Navy is ever-evolving and as new items come out for the Navy and for your designator, you have to be ready for those changes. Either adapt to the changes or retire. Don't get me wrong, I hope I am not making it seem as if I am happy with everything in the Navy, because there are certain items I disagree with, but I swore to uphold the rules, and regulations of the U.S. Navy and my superiors. Yet, what are you going to do for the rest of your career to stay competitive? You have to continue to excel in everything that you do and everything that your personnel must do. As a Mustang, you can never stop excelling and you can never stay out of date with what is expected of you. Don't ever put yourself over the mission, your Sailors, and your command, but if you don't take care of yourself, the chances of someone else taking care of you are slim. I will not say it will never occur, because I have had other LDOs take care of me, but more often than not, it does not occur. The Navy has groomed personnel to believe LDOs don't need any type of accolades or BZs, because we are LDOs and we are not here for that type of rewards. The funny thing is the command cannot continue taking from an LDO and never giving them some type of recognition, they will eventually shut down. When I mention recognition, it might mean chest candy, it might mean working with the LDO for a work schedule, it might mean taking the recommendations of the LDO, it does not just mean awards. We are Sailors just like everyone else and if you expect to take and continue receiving from Sailors they must be rewarded and recognized. We are LDOs, not machines. At the same time, do your part. Very similar to what got you here, are the same actions which will help you get promoted with the understanding that there are a few differences. Ensure your education is progressing and if you have the ability to obtain a degree do so, it will only benefit you. Second, keep your AQDs updated in your record, if you earned them, talk to your detailer as they can update your record involving AQDs. If you have the opportunity to obtain a warfare qualification, take the opportunity and if you can get two warfare insignias, don't hesitate. Lastly, sustained superior performance, your FITREPs will help you distinguish yourself above your peers, hard and soft breakouts are recommended. Continue to be well -rounded in your designator, don't just continue filling the same billet from tour to tour. If the detailer offers you different billet opportunities, don't fight the challenge, even if you feel uncomfortable. Try overseas billets, sea billets, shore billets, expeditionary billets, also consider unaccompanied billets, and special program billets to show the board you are willing to go wherever and whenever. I know there are factors which contribute to the declination of certain billets such as children in school, spouse's employment, medical situations, yet this is what will help you be placed ahead of your peers. I understand that family always comes first, but remember, someone is always hungrier.

Not selected

So, you received the "N" and this is definitely not what you were expecting. I am pretty sure you feel down in the dumps, but it is not the end of the world and, dependent on your rank and years of service, this will not be your last chance to apply. What do you do? You should be well aware if you were competitive or if you didn't have a chance of being selected. There is no question about this, but if you didn't know, if you did or didn't have a chance at being selected, then you really don't know this program. You see, you should be living and breathing this program, day in and day out. If you are not, I am not thinking you want this program bad enough. If you feel you were competitive enough but did not get selected, look over the package you submitted and see where you can improve. I have mentioned quite a few tips, not all, but plenty for your package to improve. It might be that you need that certain qualification, maybe it was a warfare that you are missing, an NEC which can assist you in being well-rounded or even a special skill such as a language, whatever it is, that may be the one item which helps you in the future. If this is your end state goal, it is just a bump in the road and not the end of the road. If you are unsure if you will be applying again next year, you probably shouldn't apply. You see, a Sailor who wants to be a Mustang will not give up until they are advised that they cannot apply any longer. Please continue and reach that goal, especially if you know you were in the competitive realm. Just don't expect to do nothing and still be selected, it might happen, but why not increase your chances. Don't forget the family, as this is a group goal, if your spouse really wants this as well, he or she will support you as they know this is beneficial for the whole family. Get those bars.

Words to the Wise (Application Tips)

To make this brief, I just want to offer some tips on what I usually tell applicants who are showing me their application prior to the local boards. This is your application, you fill it out as you wish, these are merely tips and thus far, I have helped 13 Sailors (and counting) get selected for officer programs. The majority of the application is common sense, fill in the blank information, yet there are a few items I like to see in the application. They are as follows,

-No specific block (basic items): throughout the application, ensure you are following directions with attention to detail. If the dates ask for dd/mm/yy, then double check to ensure you have 21/12/04 and not 12/21/04. If you are using all caps in a specific block, ensure the remainder of that block is the same way. Lastly, if a line is blank, one item I like to see is to place "N/A". Not a requirement, but in my mind, you have taken any possible questions out of the blank space/line. For example, block 16, if it is blank, it makes me have the question mark if the applicant forgot to place their warfare on the application, which could be a possibility, but if I see an "N/A" then I know for sure that the applicant does not have a warfare and the board member can carry on to the next step. Just an example, not picking on the applicant that does not have a warfare, just giving the example.

-blocks 20, 24, 25, and 26: If you have more items than the blocks provide for you on the application, then duplicate the specific block and add it as a separate enclosure for each block in the application. It is up to you to add these blocks, and combine the four different blocks into one sheet, I added each block as a different enclosure, so I had four enclosures, one for each of these mentioned blocks. Lastly, make sure the enclosures are in order of the application.

-block 27: In my eyes, this is one of the most important portions of the application. Why? It shows what you do during your off time and what effects each of the items had on people, the community, and Sailors. That's right, your extracurricular activity should have a cause and effect. Don't place 1) hiking 2) fishing 3) physical activity 4) running 5) hunting. Again, I am saying this because I have seen the above placed on applications. If you volunteered at Pope's Soup Kitchen, don't just state volunteer at Pope's Soup Kitchen for the homeless. Instead you can state, "Member volunteered 75 off-duty hours at Pope's Soup Kitchen serving approximately 1,500 meals to over 400 personnel which helped decrease crime in the southwest region of Alhambra County". This might be extreme, but you understand where I am coming from, ensure there is a cause and effect. Fill those five sections in this block, as a Sailor, I can guarantee you have done more than enough to fill these five sections. Show that you are human, but remember this is an application for a program.

-block 28: Whatever you do, don't place proficient in Microsoft Word, Excel, Power Point. We are in the 21st century, you tell me what Sailor in the Navy is not proficient in these programs. When I came into the Navy, even though it has not been that long, I would have understood this statement as a special skill and ability. I learned to type in the Navy, not in high school like the current generation and if you talked to my teenage kids, they have been typing and using these programs since they were in elementary school. So, what are your special skills and abilities? Are you proficient in another language? If so, that is a special skill and ensure you state exactly what you can do. In other words, state Member or "Applicant speaks, reads, writes Spanish". Additionally, do you have a certification, teach a specific course, do public speaking, instruct command indoctrination? If so, then these are your special skills. Think outside the box, these should be completed and if they relate to your designator or one you are applying for, even better. Here is one example of what I did for my application, I would teach drug detection and awareness class for a local police department. I stated on the application "Instructor for drug detection and awareness."

-blocks 29 and 30: If you happen to have one of the items in these blocks, ensure you mention them even if you had them prior to the Navy and you came in with a waiver. I had three felonies (juvenile offense) and a Driving While Intoxicated arrests on my record prior to joining which I received waivers for. I figured since the Navy had given me waivers, I should not mention them on my application. Praise God, I went to one of the LDO road shows in Naples, Italy prior to submitting and the LDO Community Manager specifically asked this question to the group and I brought up my situation, as embarrassed as I was, I spilled it out in front of my peers. He said, you have nothing to hide, place it on there, which I did and it never held me back. Again, thank you Lord! I give him all the glory, because as much as I had against me, he helped me prevail over the negatives I had self-inflicted as a teenager.

-block 35: Very simple, initial. But one of the common errors I have seen, along with the applicant signature on page 2-12.

-page 2-13: Your personal statement can be written the way you want. This is your commercial to the board and you only have 250 words, so make it good. I don't recommend this, but mine was 400 words, yes attention to detail, but I had to. I will say this, everyone states they want more "responsibility", "LDO is the pinnacle of an enlisted Sailors career", "you want to lead Sailors", and these are common statements on all the applications that I have seen. Bottom line, you have to have a hook, line and then a sinker. Catch the board and surprise them with truth and reality, not with what you think they want to hear. If you are a single parent and you want to provide everything possible to your kid that you were lacking as a kid because you were poor, then state it on there. Ensure you answer the purpose of the personal statement, which is the reason for applying, your professional and personal goals, along with strengths and personal characteristics you possess which will contribute to the success in the program you are applying for. Don't be embarrassed and don't sell yourself short.

-page 2-16: Not hard, just ensure your Commanding Officer shows he really wants to sell you to the board. Same as your personal statement, don't let the Commanding Officer be a robot stating the applicant can lead Sailors. If there is something unique about you, which can contribute to the community, ensure it is outlined in his/her statement about you. No, you can't make them write something, but you can put a bug in their ear and you can even give them a rough draft of their comments. It is up to them what they put on the application.

I will not go block-per-block on the application, but I mentioned these specific blocks, as these are the ones that usually cause headaches or challenges to the applicants. I stated on my personal statement that I wanted to pass the same aspirations I had to future Sailors, which was the end state goal of becoming a Mustang. This is why I am writing this book, to fulfill my personal statement, this book is meant to inspire you and let you know that if I was selected, you can too. There is nothing special about me, except I am that hungrier person and I have been blessed by my Lord Jesus Christ! My challenge to you is to be hungry as well!

Conclusion

So, there it is, the first book about the application involving Limited Duty Officers, and I didn't want to bore you with 200 pages of how to fill out an application. Why? Because you have certain items you must complete right now. If you are thinking about applying for the program, then you need to finalize the application, if you have been selected, then you need to prep up for the ceremony and transition to the ward room. If you have been a Mustang for one year or 30 years, then this will refresh your memories and can help you guide your reliefs. If you are a retired Mustang, you just wanted to see what this Mustang book was about and I hope you enjoyed reading it, now take that blue hat and give this book as a gift to a family member or friend who is about to join the Navy or is currently in the Navy. I know a couple of second generation Mustangs, but not many, we are few and far between and the majority of the time, other branches don't know what a Mustang is in the Navy. Hopefully, this helps educate the other branches as well. Warrants, much love to you brothers and sisters, but as much of the two programs are identical, I did not want to intertwine both of the programs, but we are all Stangs! Last advice for everyone, look for your reliefs!

Printed in the United States
By Bookmasters